# Contents

T0247537

**6** Define the term *public sector*. *[2 marks]*

..............................................................................................................................................

..............................................................................................................................................

**7** Using relevant examples, explain the difference between *needs* and *wants*. *[4 marks]*

..............................................................................................................................................

..............................................................................................................................................

..............................................................................................................................................

..............................................................................................................................................

**8** Explain the difference between *economic goods* and *free goods*. *[4 marks]*

..............................................................................................................................................

..............................................................................................................................................

..............................................................................................................................................

..............................................................................................................................................

**9** Use examples to explain how *goods* differ from *services*. *[4 marks]*

..............................................................................................................................................

..............................................................................................................................................

..............................................................................................................................................

..............................................................................................................................................

**10** Explain how poverty in the real world is an example of the basic economic problem. *[4 marks]*

..............................................................................................................................................

..............................................................................................................................................

..............................................................................................................................................

..............................................................................................................................................

# 2 The factors of production

**1** Production of any good or service requires resources known as

   **A** factors of production.             **C** production facilities.

   **B** land.                                **D** raw materials.

**2** What is the generic name for the natural resources required in the production process?

   **A** capital                      **C** labour

   **B** enterprise                  **D** land

**3** What is the name of the reward for use of enterprise in the production process?

   **A** income                    **C** rent

   **B** profit                      **D** salaries and wages

**4** Which refers to the willingness and ability of a person to relocate from one area to another for employment purposes?

   **A** geographical mobility         **C** occupational mobility

   **B** incentives to work            **D** regional unemployment

**5** What is the name given to manufactured resources required in the production process?

   **A** capital                      **C** labour

   **B** enterprise                  **D** land

**6** With the use of a relevant example, describe the meaning of *land* as a factor of production. *[2 marks]*

..................................................................................................................................................

..................................................................................................................................................

**7** Explain **two** causes of changes in the quantity and quality of factors of production. *[4 marks]*

..................................................................................................................................................

..................................................................................................................................................

..................................................................................................................................................

..................................................................................................................................................

**8 a** Explain what is meant by geographical mobility of labour as a factor resource.   *[2 marks]*

........................................................................................................................

........................................................................................................................

**b** Explain why labour, as a factor of production, is essential in the production process.   *[4 marks]*

........................................................................................................................

........................................................................................................................

........................................................................................................................

........................................................................................................................

**9** With the use of at least one example, explain how new technologies might affect the quantity and quality of factors of production in an economy.   *[4 marks]*

........................................................................................................................

........................................................................................................................

........................................................................................................................

........................................................................................................................

**10** Using relevant examples, analyse how all four factors of production are needed in the production of a good or service of your choice.   *[6 marks]*

........................................................................................................................

........................................................................................................................

........................................................................................................................

........................................................................................................................

........................................................................................................................

........................................................................................................................

........................................................................................................................

........................................................................................................................

........................................................................................................................

# 3 Opportunity cost

1  Why does almost every economic choice made have an opportunity cost?

    **A**  In most cases, there is an alternative option.

    **B**  In most cases, there is no alternative option.

    **C**  People have infinite wants.

    **D**  Resources are not allocated efficiently.

2  Which is least likely to be an opportunity cost of studying economics at university?

    **A**  other things the money could be spent on instead of going to university

    **B**  the difference in earning potential by attending university

    **C**  the option to study geography at university

    **D**  the option to work

3  From the data below, what is the opportunity cost of 1 kilogram (kg) of potatoes in terms of kilograms of carrots?

| Carrots (kg) | | Potatoes (kg) |
|---|---|---|
| 65 | plus | 25 |
| 55 | plus | 30 |

    **A**  1 kg        **B**  2 kg        **C**  5 kg        **D**  10 kg

4  From the table below, what is the opportunity cost of producing 1 extra unit of producer goods?

| Producer goods (units) | Consumer goods (units) |
|---|---|
| 30 | 52 |
| 33 | 43 |
| 36 | 34 |
| 39 | 25 |

    **A**  1 unit        **B**  3 units        **C**  6 units        **D**  9 units

5  Yann bought a new bicycle for $350 but has never used it. The second-hand value of the bicycle is $250. What is the opportunity cost to Yann of keeping the bicycle?

    **A**  $0        **B**  $100        **C**  $250        **D**  $350

**6**  Define the term *opportunity cost*.                                                                    *[2 marks]*

...................................................................................................................................................

...................................................................................................................................................

**7**  Explain the opportunity cost to society of constructing a new airport.                                *[4 marks]*

...................................................................................................................................................

...................................................................................................................................................

...................................................................................................................................................

...................................................................................................................................................

**8**  Colleen earns $10.50 an hour, but has chosen to take 2 hours off work in order to attend a school trip with her son to a theatre show. Her ticket costs $15. Calculate the opportunity cost of Colleen attending this school trip.                                *[2 marks]*

...................................................................................................................................................

...................................................................................................................................................

**9**  Sangita pays $30 for each 1-hour driving lesson taken over a 20-week period. In that time, she could have earned $18 per hour as a teaching assistant, or $12 per hour working in a local restaurant. Explain what the opportunity cost is of her taking the driving lessons.     *[2 marks]*

...................................................................................................................................................

...................................................................................................................................................

...................................................................................................................................................

...................................................................................................................................................

**10** Tiga is an outstanding 14-year-old football player who has been spotted by a top London football club. They have offered him the opportunity to play full-time, on a scholarship of £35,000 per year for the next 4 years, with the intention of becoming professional within this time. Analyse the possible opportunity costs to Tiga if he decides to take up this offer.                        *[6 marks]*

...................................................................................................................................................

...................................................................................................................................................

...................................................................................................................................................

...................................................................................................................................................

...................................................................................................................................................

...................................................................................................................................................

# 4 Production possibility curve

**1** Which does **not** shift the production possibility curve outwards?

**A** higher prices

**B** higher productivity levels

**C** improved education and healthcare

**D** technological advances

**2** What do most economies strive to increase?

**A** consumer goods

**B** opportunity cost

**C** productive capacity

**D** unemployment

**3** Which is most likely to cause an outwards shift of an economy's production possibility curve?

**A** a fall in the quality of factors of production

**B** a fall in the quantity of factors of production

**C** an increase in the quantity of factors of production

**D** higher levels of unemployment

Study the production possibility frontier diagram for Country X, which produces only two goods, wheat and oil. Use this diagram to answer Questions 4 to 6.

**4** If Country X wishes to increase the production of wheat from $W_2$ to $W_1$ the opportunity cost in terms of oil is

**A** a decrease in oil production from $O_2$ to $O_1$

**B** an increase in oil production from $O_1$ to $O_2$

**C** an outward shift of the PPF curve to point $E$

**D** $C$ to $D$

PPF diagram — Wheat (tonnes) on vertical axis, Oil (number of barrels) on horizontal axis, with points A, $W_1$, $W_2$, C, E, D, F and $O_1$, $O_2$, B marked.

**5** At which point is there spare capacity in the economy?

**A** $C$      **B** $D$      **C** $E$      **D** $F$

**6** Describe **two** ways in which Country X could increase the productive capacity of the economy and cause its PPF curve to shift outwards to point $E$. *[4 marks]*

..............................................................................................................................

..............................................................................................................................

..............................................................................................................................

..............................................................................................................................

**8** Explain **two** types of decision makers affected by microeconomics.     *[4 marks]*

..............................................................................................................................

..............................................................................................................................

..............................................................................................................................

..............................................................................................................................

..............................................................................................................................

..............................................................................................................................

**9** Explain **two** types of decision makers affected by macroeconomics.     *[4 marks]*

..............................................................................................................................

..............................................................................................................................

..............................................................................................................................

..............................................................................................................................

..............................................................................................................................

..............................................................................................................................

**10** Facebook opened a new office in central London in 2018, creating 800 jobs in the process.
The social media company first entered the UK in 2007, and earned revenue of £800 million in 2017.
The investment was welcomed, especially given the uncertainties surrounding Brexit (the UK's exit
from the European Union).

**a**  Give one reason why Facebook might have chosen to expand its operations in the UK.   *[2 marks]*

..............................................................................................................................

..............................................................................................................................

**b**  Explain **two** benefits to the British economy of Facebook's decision to invest in the UK.  *[4 marks]*

..............................................................................................................................

..............................................................................................................................

..............................................................................................................................

..............................................................................................................................

..............................................................................................................................

..............................................................................................................................

# 6 The role of markets in allocating resources

1 Changes in non-price factors that affect demand or supply will cause a change in the

   **A** equilibrium price only.        **C** quantity traded only.

   **B** equilibrium price and quantity traded.        **D** tax rate.

2 The impact of the imposition of a sales tax for a product is likely to lead to

   **A** a higher level of quantity demanded and a lower price.

   **B** a higher price and lower level of quantity demanded.

   **C** both a higher price and higher level of quantity demanded.

   **D** both a lower price and lower level of quantity demanded.

3 Which is **not** a supply factor that causes a change in the equilibrium price of a product?

   **A** price changes        **C** spare capacity

   **B** sales taxes        **D** subsidies

4 Which is a consequence of lower demand for a particular product?

   **A** Equilibrium quantity falls and the price falls.    **C** Equilibrium quantity rises and the price falls.

   **B** Equilibrium quantity falls and the price rises.    **D** Equilibrium quantity rises and the price rises.

5 Which will cause a rightwards shift of the demand curve?

   **A** higher production costs        **C** lower sales taxes

   **B** lower income taxes        **D** subsidies provided to producers

6 State **two** factors that can shift the demand curve for a good or service.    *[2 marks]*

   ................................................................................................................................................

   ................................................................................................................................................

7 'Price changes can occur due to shifts in demand or supply.' Explain what this statement means.    *[4 marks]*

   ................................................................................................................................................

   ................................................................................................................................................

   ................................................................................................................................................

   ................................................................................................................................................

8  Explain **two** reasons why the demand for foreign holidays might increase.          *[4 marks]*

....................................................................................................

....................................................................................................

....................................................................................................

....................................................................................................

....................................................................................................

....................................................................................................

9  Explain **two** reasons for a leftwards shift of the supply curve of avocados.          *[4 marks]*

....................................................................................................

....................................................................................................

....................................................................................................

....................................................................................................

....................................................................................................

10  Using an appropriate demand and supply diagram, explain the impact on the market for electric cars following a government announcement to subsidise the purchase of such vehicles.          *[4 marks]*

....................................................................................................

....................................................................................................

....................................................................................................

....................................................................................................

....................................................................................................

....................................................................................................

                    *Cambridge IGCSE™ and O Level Economics 2nd edition Workbook*

# 7 Demand

1 The willingness and ability of customers to pay a given price to buy a good or service is known as

   **A** effective demand.              **C** quantity demanded.

   **B** market demand.                **D** the law of demand.

2 Which statement explains why there might be a decrease in the demand for sugar?

   **A** Consumers are more aware of health issues related to sugar.

   **B** Demand for coffee and tea has increased.

   **C** New technologies increase the output of sugar.

   **D** There is an increase in the supply of land to produce sugar.

3 Which factor does **not** explain why the demand for cars in China has continuously increased?

   **A** effective advertising and marketing from car makers

   **B** greater household disposable incomes

   **C** higher interest rates in China

   **D** lower import taxes on cars made outside of China

4 Which products are considered to be complementary goods?

   **A** apples and oranges            **C** sugar and tea

   **B** shampoo and conditioner      **D** tea and coffee

5 Which is **not** a determinant of demand?

   **A** income                    **C** subsidies

   **B** price                      **D** substitutes

6 Explain why an ordinary demand curve is downwards sloping. *[2 marks]*

........................................................................................................................................

........................................................................................................................................

**8** Explain **two** factors that might shift the supply curve of motor vehicles.          *[4 marks]*

.......................................................................................................................

.......................................................................................................................

.......................................................................................................................

.......................................................................................................................

**9** Using an appropriate supply diagram, explain the impact on the supply of textbooks
following subsidies being awarded to educational publishers.          *[4 marks]*

.......................................................................................................................

.......................................................................................................................

.......................................................................................................................

.......................................................................................................................

**10** Use an appropriate diagram to analyse how the imposition of a tax on suppliers of
oil (petrol) affects the quantity supplied.          *[6 marks]*

.......................................................................................................................

.......................................................................................................................

.......................................................................................................................

.......................................................................................................................

.......................................................................................................................

.......................................................................................................................

# 9 Price determination

**1** The position where the demand for a product is equal to the supply of the product is known as

**A** demand.

**C** market equilibrium.

**B** equilibrium price.

**D** supply.

**2** What exists when there are shortages or surpluses in a market?

**A** excess demand

**C** market disequilibrium

**B** excess supply

**D** market equilibrium

**3** What occurs when the demand for a product exceeds the supply of the product due to the price being lower than the market equilibrium?

**A** excess supply

**C** shortage

**B** market equilibrium

**D** surplus

**4** Which situation exists when the price is set above the market equilibrium price, thus creating a surplus in the market?

**A** excess demand

**C** market disequilibrium

**B** excess supply

**D** market equilibrium

**5** The data below shows the demand and supply schedule for mushrooms each week. Which of the statements below is incorrect?

| Supply | Price per unit ($) | Demand |
|---|---|---|
| 21 000 | 10 | 18 000 |
| 20 000 | 9 | 20 000 |
| 19 000 | 8 | 22 000 |

**A** At $8 per unit, there is excess demand of 3000 units.

**B** At $10 per unit, there is excess supply of 3000 units.

**C** Equilibrium exists at $9 per unit.

**D** There is a shortage in the market at $10 per unit.

**6** Define the term *market equilibrium*. *[2 marks]*

..................................................................................................................................................

..................................................................................................................................................

**7** Using appropriate examples, explain the difference between a shortage and a surplus.    *[4 marks]*

.............................................................................................................................................

.............................................................................................................................................

.............................................................................................................................................

.............................................................................................................................................

**8** Explain the difference between equilibrium price and disequilibrium price.    *[4 marks]*

.............................................................................................................................................

.............................................................................................................................................

.............................................................................................................................................

.............................................................................................................................................

**9** With the aid of a diagram, explain what is meant by excess demand.    *[4 marks]*

.............................................................................................................................................

.............................................................................................................................................

**10** Use an appropriate diagram to analyse how the imposition of a tax on suppliers of oil (petrol) affects the market equilibrium price and quantity traded.    *[6 marks]*

.............................................................................................................................................

.............................................................................................................................................

.............................................................................................................................................

.............................................................................................................................................

# 10 Price changes

1 Which is the most probable outcome if a government raises the tax on the sale of cigarettes and tobacco?

   **A** higher price and higher quantity traded       **C** lower price and higher quantity traded

   **B** higher price and lower quantity traded       **D** lower price and lower quantity traded

2 Which factor below would **not** cause a rightwards shift of the supply curve for the agricultural sector?

   **A** government subsidies for farmers       **C** technological progress in agriculture

   **B** favourable weather conditions       **D** higher costs of fertilisers

3 Which of the factors below would **not** cause a rightwards shift of the demand curve for petrol cars?

   **A** effective persuasive advertising       **C** imposition of a new vehicle registration tax

   **B** higher disposable household income       **D** significantly higher prices of electric cars

4 What is the general outcome if there is excess demand in a market?

   **A** The price falls.       **C** The price falls but demand rises.

   **B** The price rises.       **D** The quantity traded rises.

5 What is most likely to occur in the market for Nike sports shoes following a fall in price of Adidas sports shoes?

   **A** Quantity demanded falls.       **C** The price falls and quantity demanded rises.

   **B** Quantity demanded rises.       **D** The price rises and quantity demanded falls.

6 State **two** factors that would cause the supply curve for a product to shift to the left.    *[2 marks]*

   ........................................................................................................................

   ........................................................................................................................

7 Give one reason why technological progress might increase prices, and one reason why it might cause prices to fall.    *[2 marks]*

   ........................................................................................................................

   ........................................................................................................................

6 Suppose HTC sells 8000 smartphones in Taiwan per week at a price of $250. Due to competition, HTC reduces the price to $225 and subsequently notices that demand for its smartphones increases to 8640 units in the following week.

a Calculate the price elasticity of demand for HTC smartphones. *[2 marks]*

..............................................................................................................................

..............................................................................................................................

b Explain whether it was a good decision for HTC to reduce its price. *[4 marks]*

..............................................................................................................................

..............................................................................................................................

..............................................................................................................................

..............................................................................................................................

7 The price elasticity of demand (PED) for cigarettes in a particular country is known to be –0.55.

a Describe what would happen to the demand for cigarettes if the price of cigarettes increases by 10%. *[2 marks]*

..............................................................................................................................

..............................................................................................................................

b Explain one factor which affects the PED for cigarettes. *[2 marks]*

..............................................................................................................................

..............................................................................................................................

8 Analyse how an airline company can use the concept of price elasticity of demand to decide whether or not to reduce its air fares. *[6 marks]*

..............................................................................................................................

..............................................................................................................................

..............................................................................................................................

..............................................................................................................................

..............................................................................................................................

..............................................................................................................................

**9** Shanchez Sunglasses sells 240 pairs of its best-selling sunglasses at $250 each per month. Following an increase in price to $280, Shanchez Sunglasses discovers that the quantity demanded falls to 215 units per month.

   **a** Calculate the price elasticity of demand for Shanchez Sunglasses' best-selling sunglasses. *[2 marks]*

..........................................................................................................................

..........................................................................................................................

..........................................................................................................................

..........................................................................................................................

..........................................................................................................................

..........................................................................................................................

   **b** Using your answer from Question 9a above, explain how knowledge of price elasticity of demand (PED) can be of use to Shanchez Sunglasses. *[4 marks]*

..........................................................................................................................

..........................................................................................................................

..........................................................................................................................

..........................................................................................................................

..........................................................................................................................

..........................................................................................................................

**10** With the use of appropriate examples, analyse the factors that determine the value of price elasticity of demand (PED). *[6 marks]*

..........................................................................................................................

..........................................................................................................................

..........................................................................................................................

..........................................................................................................................

..........................................................................................................................

..........................................................................................................................

..........................................................................................................................

..........................................................................................................................

**9** Explain why there is greater inequality in income and wealth distribution in a market economic system than in a mixed economic system. *[4 marks]*

..........................................................................................................................................

..........................................................................................................................................

..........................................................................................................................................

..........................................................................................................................................

..........................................................................................................................................

..........................................................................................................................................

**10** Discuss whether most people living in a market economic system (free market economy) benefit from such an economic system. *[8 marks]*

..........................................................................................................................................

..........................................................................................................................................

..........................................................................................................................................

..........................................................................................................................................

..........................................................................................................................................

..........................................................................................................................................

..........................................................................................................................................

..........................................................................................................................................

..........................................................................................................................................

..........................................................................................................................................

..........................................................................................................................................

..........................................................................................................................................

..........................................................................................................................................

# 14 Market failure

**1** Which is **not** an example of market failure?

   **A** air pollution

   **B** a supermarket charging high prices because of its monopoly power

   **C** car parks in a town centre

   **D** congestion caused by the number of cars on the road

**2** Which is an example of a public good?

   **A** healthcare                **C** public fireworks display

   **B** museums                 **D** public playgrounds

**3** A government decides to build another airport terminal at an existing airport. This will increase air and road traffic around the airport but will also increase trade and tourism and create business and employment opportunities. Which economic concepts are mentioned in the above statements?

   **A** conservation of resources, economic growth, external benefits

   **B** external costs, external benefits, opportunity cost

   **C** external costs, opportunity cost, conservation of resources

   **D** opportunity cost, occupational mobility of labour, geographical mobility

**4** Which is **not** a characteristic of a merit good?

   **A** over-provided             **C** under-consumed

   **B** provides social benefits      **D** under-provided

**5** Which does **not** provide external benefits to society?

   **A** a local college that provides education and training to increase people's skills and qualifications

   **B** a new history museum

   **C** a public park

   **D** new public housing funded by the government

**6** Give **two** examples of goods and/or services that are provided by a government because they would otherwise be under-consumed by society.     *[2 marks]*

.................................................................................................................................................

.................................................................................................................................................

7   The development of Macau, a Special Administrative Region of China, as an entertainment
    centre has brought mass tourism and many job opportunities to the region. The construction
    of hotels has required reclamation of the sea, a loss of vegetation and areas of natural
    beauty and a loss of local culture. Explain **two** examples of market failure which have
    occurred in Macau.                                                          *[4 marks]*

    .............................................................................................................

    .............................................................................................................

    .............................................................................................................

    .............................................................................................................

    .............................................................................................................

8   Explain why governments provide public goods.                             *[4 marks]*

    .............................................................................................................

    .............................................................................................................

    .............................................................................................................

    .............................................................................................................

    .............................................................................................................

9   The construction of the Three Gorges Dam in China cost $37 billion. It is the world's largest
    power station. Over 1 million people were relocated because their homes were destroyed
    during the construction of the dam and many farmers lost their livelihoods (means of earning
    income) because they lost their land. Discuss the social costs and social benefits of the
    construction of the Three Gorges Dam.                                      *[8 marks]*

    .............................................................................................................

    .............................................................................................................

    .............................................................................................................

    .............................................................................................................

    .............................................................................................................

    .............................................................................................................

    .............................................................................................................

    .............................................................................................................

    .............................................................................................................

**10** Students in the USA, Canada and England have to pay to go to university. In Sweden and Scotland, the governments fund university education because of the perceived social benefits.

**a** Define what is meant by *social benefits*. *[2 marks]*

..............................................................................................................................

..............................................................................................................................

**b** Explain **two** advantages of charging people for a university education. *[4 marks]*

..............................................................................................................................

..............................................................................................................................

..............................................................................................................................

..............................................................................................................................

..............................................................................................................................

..............................................................................................................................

**c** Discuss whether or not subsidising university education will benefit society. *[8 marks]*

..............................................................................................................................

..............................................................................................................................

..............................................................................................................................

..............................................................................................................................

..............................................................................................................................

..............................................................................................................................

..............................................................................................................................

..............................................................................................................................

..............................................................................................................................

..............................................................................................................................

..............................................................................................................................

..............................................................................................................................

# 16 Money and banking

1 Which is **not** a function of money?

   **A** durability

   **B** measure of value

   **C** medium of exchange

   **D** store of value

2 Which is **not** a problem of bartering as a medium of exchange?

   **A** the need for a double coincidence of wants

   **B** the need for divisibility

   **C** the need for portability

   **D** the need for trade and exchange

3 Which is **not** a function of a central bank?

   **A** the facilitation of company growth

   **B** the government's bank

   **C** the lender of last resort

   **D** the sole issuer of bank notes and coins in the country

4 Which is a secondary function of commercial banks?

   **A** accepting deposits

   **B** credit creation

   **C** making advances

   **D** offering internet banking

5 Which are **not** functions of a commercial bank?

   **A** cheque clearance and foreign exchange dealings

   **B** internet banking and money transfer facilities

   **C** lender of the last resort and bankers' bank

   **D** loans and credit creation

6 'Money acts as a medium of exchange.' Explain what this means. *[4 marks]*

........................................................................................................................

........................................................................................................................

........................................................................................................................

........................................................................................................................

........................................................................................................................

        *Cambridge IGCSE™ and O Level Economics 2nd edition Workbook*

**7** Explain **two** reasons why bank notes and coins are used as money. *[4 marks]*

.........................................................................................................................................

.........................................................................................................................................

.........................................................................................................................................

.........................................................................................................................................

**8** Explain **two** functions of a central bank. *[4 marks]*

.........................................................................................................................................

.........................................................................................................................................

.........................................................................................................................................

.........................................................................................................................................

**9** Explain **two** functions of commercial banks. *[4 marks]*

.........................................................................................................................................

.........................................................................................................................................

.........................................................................................................................................

.........................................................................................................................................

**10** In some countries people can pay for goods and services using an app on their smartphone, for example Apple Pay or Android Pay. Discuss whether or not these payment apps are a new form of money. *[8 marks]*

.........................................................................................................................................

.........................................................................................................................................

.........................................................................................................................................

.........................................................................................................................................

.........................................................................................................................................

.........................................................................................................................................

.........................................................................................................................................

.........................................................................................................................................

.........................................................................................................................................

.........................................................................................................................................

# 17 Households

**1** What is the main source of income for most people?

   **A** dividends                        **C** profit

   **B** interest                          **D** wages and salaries

**2** Which term describes income earned by an individual after income tax and other charges have been deducted?

   **A** disposable income            **C** nominal income

   **B** gross income                   **D** real income

**3** Money intended for spending on goods and services within the next twelve months is known as

   **A** capital                        **C** current expenditure

   **B** capital expenditure          **D** savings

**4** Which type of consumption occurs when people buy goods and services that they feel increase their social status or image?

   **A** capital consumption         **C** current consumption

   **B** conspicuous consumption    **D** household consumption

**5** Which is the least likely determinant of the level of spending, saving and borrowing in an economy?

   **A** consumer confidence levels    **C** interest rates

   **B** inflation rates                   **D** trade policies

**6** Define the term *wealth*.                                        *[2 marks]*

...........................................................................................................................................

...........................................................................................................................................

**7** State **two** factors that determine the level of savings in an economy.     *[2 marks]*

...........................................................................................................................................

...........................................................................................................................................

                                   *Cambridge IGCSE™ and O Level Economics 2nd edition Workbook*

**8** Explain **two** reasons why an individual might choose to borrow money. *[4 marks]*

..................................................................................................................

..................................................................................................................

..................................................................................................................

..................................................................................................................

**9** Explain how the use of interest rates affects the amount of spending and savings in an economy. *[4 marks]*

..................................................................................................................

..................................................................................................................

..................................................................................................................

..................................................................................................................

**10** Some countries, such as Belgium and France, impose high rates of income tax. Explain how direct taxes impact on the amount a person saves or spends. *[4 marks]*

..................................................................................................................

..................................................................................................................

..................................................................................................................

..................................................................................................................

# 20 Firms

1 Which sector of the economy contains firms that provide services to the general public and other firms?

   **A** primary                        **C** secondary

   **B** public                         **D** tertiary

2 Which is **not** a method used to measure the size of firms?

   **A** costs of production            **C** sales revenue

   **B** market share                 **D** the number of employees

3 Which is **not** an advantage of small firms?

   **A** easier to set up                **C** opportunities to gain economies of scale

   **B** greater degree of control     **D** quicker decision making

4 Which type of growth occurs when firms expand using their own resources?

   **A** external                    **C** mergers and acquisitions

   **B** inorganic                   **D** organic

5 Which type of economies of scale arise due to the location of the firm?

   **A** external                    **C** internal

   **B** financial                   **D** risk-bearing

6 Define the term *diseconomies of scale*.               *[2 marks]*

..................................................................................................................................

..................................................................................................................................

..................................................................................................................................

7 Give **two** examples of external economies of scale.       *[2 marks]*

..................................................................................................................................

..................................................................................................................................

8 McDonald's uses franchising to grow its business. Define the term *franchise*.    *[2 marks]*

..................................................................................................................................

..................................................................................................................................

                       *Cambridge IGCSE™ and O Level Economics 2nd edition Workbook*

**9** Explain the difference between backward and forward vertical integration. *[4 marks]*

**10** Explain **two** disadvantages of (challenges facing) small firms. *[4 marks]*

# 21 Firms and production

1  Which is **not** a factor of production?

   **A**  enterprise                    **C**  land

   **B**  labour                        **D**  money

2  The production of which goods or services is least likely to be labour-intensive?

   **A**  a Hollywood movie             **C**  carbonated soft drinks

   **B**  a made-to-measure wedding dress   **D**  private piano lessons

3  Which economic term is used to describe or measure how well resources are used in the production process?

   **A**  competitiveness               **C**  innovation

   **B**  economies of scale            **D**  productivity

4  The commercialisation of new ideas and products as an essential source of productivity is known as

   **A**  efficiency.                    **C**  innovation.

   **B**  entrepreneurial spirit.        **D**  productivity.

5  The demand for factors of production is dependent on the demand for the goods and services which they will be used to produce. This concept is known as

   **A**  competitiveness.               **C**  factor inputs.

   **B**  derived demand.                **D**  investment.

6  Define the term *capital-intensive production*.                                    *[2 marks]*

   ..............................................................................................................................................

   ..............................................................................................................................................

7  'The demand for factors of production (land, labour, capital and enterprise) is derived in demand.'
   Explain what this means.                                                           *[2 marks]*

   ..............................................................................................................................................

   ..............................................................................................................................................

   ..............................................................................................................................................

   ..............................................................................................................................................

                               *Cambridge IGCSE™ and O Level Economics 2nd edition Workbook*

**8** Explain how productivity can improve due to an increase in investment expenditure in the economy. *[4 marks]*

..................................................................................................................................

..................................................................................................................................

..................................................................................................................................

..................................................................................................................................

**9** Study the data below for two car sales firms over a typical month. The sales revenue for each firm is shown, as well as the number of cars sold and the number of sales staff involved.

| Firm | Sales revenue ($) | Cars sold | Sales staff |
|---|---|---|---|
| Morganics Cars | 284 850 | 15 | 5 |
| Agent Cars | 366 440 | 30 | 8 |

**a** Calculate the labour productivity as measured by the monthly sales per worker for both Morganics Cars and Agent Cars. *[2 marks]*

..................................................................................................................................

..................................................................................................................................

**b** Describe your findings. *[2 marks]*

..................................................................................................................................

..................................................................................................................................

**c** Explain why it might be difficult to determine whether Morganics Cars or Agent Cars is the more productive firm. *[4 marks]*

..................................................................................................................................

..................................................................................................................................

..................................................................................................................................

..................................................................................................................................

**10** Using relevant examples, explain why productivity is vital for the survival of firms. *[4 marks]*

..................................................................................................................................

..................................................................................................................................

..................................................................................................................................

..................................................................................................................................

..................................................................................................................................

# 22 Firms' costs, revenue and objectives

**1** Which is a fixed cost of production for a manufacturing firm?

    **A** electricity charges             **C** rental payments

    **B** overtime pay                  **D** workers' wages

**2** What is the term used to describe the costs of production that have to be paid regardless of how much a firm produces or sells?

    **A** average                  **C** total

    **B** fixed                     **D** variable

**3** What is the correct label for the upwards sloping line shown in the graph below?

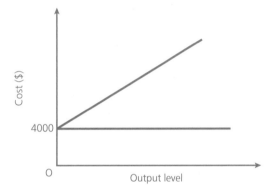

    **A** average costs

    **B** fixed costs

    **C** total costs

    **D** variable costs

**4** A firm's variable costs are $20 000 in a given week when its output is 2000 units, while fixed costs are $10 000. What is the value of the firm's average costs?

    **A** $5             **B** $10             **C** $15             **D** $20

**5** The payment received by a firm from the sale of its goods and/or services is known as

    **A** income                 **C** salaries

    **B** revenue                **D** total costs

**6** The diagram below shows economies of scale. Identify appropriate labels to complete the diagram. *[2 marks]*

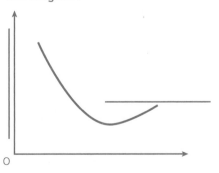

**7** The table below shows a firm's fixed and variable costs of production at different levels of output. Calculate the level of output where average costs are at their lowest. *[2 marks]*

| Output (units) | Fixed costs ($) | Variable costs ($) | Total costs ($) | Average costs ($) |
|---|---|---|---|---|
| 100 | 2000 | 400 | | |
| 200 | 2000 | 760 | | |
| 300 | 2000 | 1200 | | |
| 400 | 2000 | 2320 | | |

..............................................................................................................................

..............................................................................................................................

..............................................................................................................................

**8** The table below shows the total costs of a firm at different levels of output. It sells each unit for $20.

| Quantity produced (units) | 20 | 30 | 40 | 50 |
|---|---|---|---|---|
| Total cost ($) | 200 | 285 | 360 | 460 |
| Average cost ($) | | | | |

**a** Calculate the level of output required to minimise average costs. *[2 marks]*

..............................................................................................................................

..............................................................................................................................

..............................................................................................................................

**b** Calculate how many units the firm needs to produce and sell in order to maximise profits. *[2 marks]*

..............................................................................................................................

..............................................................................................................................

..............................................................................................................................

**9** Study the data for a firm below and answer the questions that follow.

| Output (tonnes) | Total cost ($) | Total revenue ($) |
|---|---|---|
| 0 | 1000 | 0 |
| 100 | 2000 | 1500 |
| 200 | 2800 | 3000 |
| 300 | 3700 | 4500 |
| 400 | 5200 | 6000 |

**a** Calculate the unit price from the data above. *[2 marks]*

..............................................................................................................................

**b** Calculate the level of output at which average costs are minimised for the firm. *[2 marks]*

..................................................................................................................

..................................................................................................................

..................................................................................................................

**c** Calculate the profit at each level of output. *[2 marks]*

| Output (tonnes) | Total cost ($) | Total revenue ($) | Profit ($) |
|---|---|---|---|
| 0 | 1000 | 0 | |
| 100 | 2000 | 1500 | |
| 200 | 2800 | 3000 | |
| 300 | 3700 | 4500 | |
| 400 | 5200 | 6000 | |

..................................................................................................................

..................................................................................................................

..................................................................................................................

**10** Nina's Bakery has fixed costs of $8000 each month. The firm's average variable costs are $3 per unit of output. The current level of demand at Nina's Bakery is 20 500 units per month. The average price of its products is $5.50.

**a** Calculate the monthly total costs of production at Nina's Bakery. *[2 marks]*

..................................................................................................................

..................................................................................................................

**b** Calculate the current average costs each month for Nina's Bakery. *[2 marks]*

..................................................................................................................

..................................................................................................................

**c** Calculate the profit if demand at Nina's Bakery increases to 25 000 units per month. *[2 marks]*

..................................................................................................................

..................................................................................................................

..................................................................................................................

*Cambridge IGCSE™ and O Level Economics 2nd edition Workbook*

# 23 Market structure

1 Which is **not** a characteristic of firms in a highly competitive market?

A  barriers to entry

B  differentiated products

C  many buyers and sellers

D  non-price competition

2 Which characteristic is **not** relevant to the model of monopoly?

A  extreme barriers to entry

B  price setter

C  price taker

D  sole supplier

3 Which is least likely to be an entry barrier to the publishing industry?

A  consumer protection laws

B  economies of scale enjoyed by the leading publishing firms

C  existing publishers with established market share

D  set-up costs

4 Which term is used to describe the market structure where only one supplier of a good or service exists?

A  market leader

B  monopoly

C  price maker

D  price setter

5 Which is **not** a key characteristic of a market?

A  degree and intensity of price and non-price competition

B  nature of barriers to entry

C  number of firms in the market

D  number of price takers and makers

6 Define the term *market structure*. *[2 marks]*

..............................................................................................................................................

..............................................................................................................................................

7 Explain **two** disadvantages of monopoly. *[4 marks]*

..............................................................................................................................................

..............................................................................................................................................

..............................................................................................................................................

..............................................................................................................................................

**8** Explain why a government aims to redistribute income in the economy. *[4 marks]*

..............................................................................................................

..............................................................................................................

..............................................................................................................

..............................................................................................................

..............................................................................................................

**9** Explain why price stability is a key government aim. *[4 marks]*

..............................................................................................................

..............................................................................................................

..............................................................................................................

..............................................................................................................

..............................................................................................................

**10** In some countries, governments use subsidies to reduce the impact of inflation.

**a** Define the term *subsidy*. *[2 marks]*

..............................................................................................................

..............................................................................................................

..............................................................................................................

**b** Define the term *inflation*. *[2 marks]*

..............................................................................................................

..............................................................................................................

..............................................................................................................

**c** Explain how the use of subsidies can help to reduce inflation. *[4 marks]*

..............................................................................................................

..............................................................................................................

..............................................................................................................

..............................................................................................................

..............................................................................................................

# 26 Fiscal policy

1 What is the term used to describe taxes paid from the income, wealth and profits of individuals and firms?

  **A**  corporation tax           **C**  income tax

  **B**  direct tax                  **D**  indirect tax

2 If a government loosens fiscal policy in an attempt to expand the economy, what does this involve?

  **A**  raising taxes and raising government expenditure

  **B**  raising taxes and reducing government expenditure

  **C**  reducing taxes and raising government expenditure

  **D**  reducing taxes and reducing government expenditure

3 A government aims to expand aggregate demand in the economy to boost national output and employment. Which policy should it use?

  **A**  raise expenditure on education and healthcare

  **B**  raise taxes and raise interest rates

  **C**  reduce government spending and raise taxes

  **D**  reduce taxes and reduce interest rates

4 Which statement does **not** outline how fiscal policy can be used to reduce unemployment in the economy?

  **A**  A cut in taxes may increase consumer spending.

  **B**  Government spending can create jobs in both the private and public sectors.

  **C**  Greater government spending increases aggregate demand, causing the derived demand for labour to rise.

  **D**  Lower interest rates increase the spending ability of households and encourage firms to invest more.

5 When does a budget surplus occur?

  **A**  when a country exports more than it imports

  **B**  when a country imports more than it exports

  **C**  when government revenues exceed public expenditure

  **D**  when public expenditure exceeds government revenues

**6** Explain **two** reasons why the government might choose to increase public expenditure in the economy. *[4 marks]*

..........................................................................................................................

..........................................................................................................................

..........................................................................................................................

..........................................................................................................................

..........................................................................................................................

**7** The Bahamas and Estonia have a zero rate of corporation tax. Explain **two** reasons behind such a government decision. *[4 marks]*

..........................................................................................................................

..........................................................................................................................

..........................................................................................................................

..........................................................................................................................

..........................................................................................................................

**8** Suppose in a country the progressive tax rates are 12% (for those earning between $10 001 and $50 000 per year) and 17% (for those earning over $50 000 per year).

**a** Complete the table below and calculate the total amount of tax paid by an individual who earns $80 000 a year. *[2 marks]*

| Income level ($) | Tax rate (%) | Amount of tax paid ($) |
|---|---|---|
| $10 000 | 0% | |
| $10 001–$50 000 | 12% | |
| $50 000+ | 17% | |
| Total tax: | | |

**b** Calculate the average rate of income tax paid by the individual. *[2 marks]*

..........................................................................................................................

..........................................................................................................................

**9 a** Define the term *supply-side policy*. *[2 marks]*

..........................................................................................................................

..........................................................................................................................

**b** Analyse how fiscal policy can impact on the supply-side of an economy. *[6 marks]*

**10 a** Define the term *contractionary fiscal policy*. *[2 marks]*

**b** Discuss whether raising income taxes is in the best interest of the economy. *[8 marks]*

# 29 Economic growth

**1** Economic growth can be defined as

    **A**  an increase in a country's exports earnings.

    **B**  an increase in a country's potential earnings.

    **C**  an increase in the productive capacity of an economy.

    **D**  a reduction in the cost of living.

**2** Whether a country has experienced economic growth is best indicated by an increase in

    **A**  consumer price inflation.

    **B**  current account on the balance of payments.

    **C**  employment.

    **D**  real GDP per capita.

**3** As a country experiences economic growth, what is likely to fall?

    **A**  average years of schooling

    **B**  employment opportunities

    **C**  infant mortality rates

    **D**  national income per capita

**4** Which is most likely to be a concern about rapid economic growth in a country?

    **A**  higher costs of production

    **B**  higher tax revenues

    **C**  increased demand for imports

    **D**  resource depletion

**5** Which is **not** a policy used to promote economic growth?

    **A**  increase spending on education

    **B**  lower government spending

    **C**  lower income tax rates

    **D**  lower interest rates

*Cambridge IGCSE™ and O Level Economics 2nd edition Workbook*

**6** Define the term *recession*. [2 marks]

......................................................................................................................................

......................................................................................................................................

......................................................................................................................................

**7** Explain how a country's net exports are calculated. [2 marks]

......................................................................................................................................

......................................................................................................................................

......................................................................................................................................

**8** Explain **two** causes of economic growth. [4 marks]

......................................................................................................................................

......................................................................................................................................

......................................................................................................................................

......................................................................................................................................

......................................................................................................................................

**9** The diagram below shows a typical business cycle. Identify appropriate labels to complete the diagram. [3 marks]

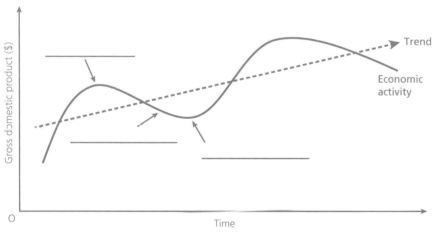

**10** Diaby, an entrepreneur, opened an internet café in a village in Ghana equipped with ten computers and wi-fi for customer use. The café is very popular with students, farmers and people in the village who run or would like to run their own businesses. Farmers use it to research information about new farming techniques and where to get the best market price for their produce. Other villagers use it to find out about installing solar power and how to access funds available for financing new and existing businesses. Diaby organises computing classes and displays useful information about energy saving and new planting techniques on the café notice board.

**a** Using a PPC curve, explain the impact of the internet café on the output of the village. *[4 marks]*

..................................................................................................................................

..................................................................................................................................

..................................................................................................................................

..................................................................................................................................

**b** Explain **two** reasons why output in the village has increased as a result of the internet. *[4 marks]*

..................................................................................................................................

..................................................................................................................................

..................................................................................................................................

..................................................................................................................................

..................................................................................................................................

..................................................................................................................................

# 30 Employment and unemployment

1 What is the name given to the situation when people of working age are both willing and able to work but cannot find employment?

A classical unemployment      C unemployment rate

B unemployment      D voluntary unemployment

2 Which type of government policy is best suited to deal with imperfections in the labour market?

A fiscal policies      C protectionist policies

B monetary policies      D supply-side policies

3 Which is generally regarded as the most severe form of unemployment?

A cyclical unemployment      C structural unemployment

B real wage unemployment      D voluntary unemployment

4 The table below gives population data for a particular country.

| Population: | 66 million |
|---|---|
| Aged 0–14: | 17 million |
| Aged 15–64: | 38 million |
| Aged over 65: | 11 million |

If the unemployment rate is 7%, the number of unemployed people is

A 2.66 million      C 10 million

B 4.62 million      D 28 million

5 What is the main cause of frictional unemployment?

A changes in demand for certain goods and services

B people changing jobs

C people choosing not to work

D wages set higher than the market equilibrium

6 Explain what is meant by the unemployment rate.      *[2 marks]*

......................................................................................................................................

......................................................................................................................................

**7** Calculate the unemployment rate in a country that has a population of 46.6 million people, of which 30 million are employed and 2.7 million are unemployed. *[2 marks]*

.....................................................................................................................................

.....................................................................................................................................

.....................................................................................................................................

**8** Explain which type of unemployment is most associated with a downturn in the business cycle. *[2 marks]*

.....................................................................................................................................

.....................................................................................................................................

.....................................................................................................................................

**9** Explain how the International Labour Organization measures unemployment. *[2 marks]*

.....................................................................................................................................

.....................................................................................................................................

.....................................................................................................................................

.....................................................................................................................................

**10** Explain **two** economic advantages of a fall in unemployment. *[4 marks]*

.....................................................................................................................................

.....................................................................................................................................

.....................................................................................................................................

.....................................................................................................................................

.....................................................................................................................................

.....................................................................................................................................

# 31 Inflation and deflation

1  Which will cause an increase in a country's rate of inflation?

   **A**  discount food prices at the major supermarkets

   **B**  lower consumer and business confidence in the economy

   **C**  lower rates of interest

   **D**  subsidised energy prices

2  Which statement suggests why savers lose out during times of inflation?

   **A**  Money loses its ability to act as a store of value.

   **B**  Money loses its ability to act as a unit of account.

   **C**  Real interest rates become negative during inflationary periods.

   **D**  Real interest rates become positive during inflationary periods.

3  If the weighting for food in a country's consumer price index (CPI) exceeds that for shoes, what does this indicate?

   **A**  Food is considered to be more important to the average household than shoes.

   **B**  On average, the price of food has increased more than the price of shoes.

   **C**  The average household buys more food than shoes.

   **D**  The average household buys more shoes than food.

4  If the consumer price index in a country rises from 115.2 to 116.8 in the subsequent year, what is the inflation rate?

   **A**  1.39%                         **C**  1.68%

   **B**  1.6%                          **D**  16.8%

5  The tables below show the consumer price index (CPI) data.

| Year | CPI |
|------|------|
| 1 | 102.2 |
| 2 | 104.6 |

| Year | CPI |
|------|------|
| 3 | 103.9 |
| 4 | 105.4 |

   It can be concluded that prices were at their lowest in

   **A**  Year 1                        **C**  Year 3

   **B**  Year 2                        **D**  Year 4

**6** Calculate the rate of inflation if the consumer price index drops from 135.6 to 130.2.  *[2 marks]*

.......................................................................................................................................

.......................................................................................................................................

.......................................................................................................................................

.......................................................................................................................................

**7** A basket of goods and services currently costs $1500. Calculate how much it would cost if the consumer price index fell from 125.5 to 121.1.  *[2 marks]*

.......................................................................................................................................

.......................................................................................................................................

.......................................................................................................................................

.......................................................................................................................................

**8** Explain **two** reasons why governments calculate a consumer price index.  *[4 marks]*

.......................................................................................................................................

.......................................................................................................................................

.......................................................................................................................................

.......................................................................................................................................

.......................................................................................................................................

.......................................................................................................................................

**9** Explain why food and furniture have different weightings when calculating the consumer price index.  *[4 marks]*

.......................................................................................................................................

.......................................................................................................................................

.......................................................................................................................................

.......................................................................................................................................

.......................................................................................................................................

.......................................................................................................................................

**10** The data below is for a hypothetical country, Satcolbe.

| Item | Retail prices index | Weight |
|---|---|---|
| Clothing | 120 | 15 |
| Food | 130 | 30 |
| Housing | 140 | 40 |
| Other | 125 | 15 |

   **a**  Define what is meant by a *retail prices index* (RPI).           *[2 marks]*

......................................................................................................................................................

......................................................................................................................................................

......................................................................................................................................................

   **b**  'The typical household in Satcolbe spends more money on food than on clothing.'
      Explain this statement.           *[2 marks]*

......................................................................................................................................................

......................................................................................................................................................

......................................................................................................................................................

   **c**  Complete the table below and calculate the weighted retail prices index
      (RPI) in Satcolbe.           *[2 marks]*

| Item | Retail prices index | Weight | Weighted index |
|---|---|---|---|
| Clothing | 120 | 15 | |
| Food | 130 | 30 | |
| Housing | 140 | 40 | |
| Other | 125 | 15 | |
| Weighted RPI | | | |

# 32 Living standards

1 Which factor is **not** an indicator used to measure poverty within a country?

   **A** high cost of living

   **B** high mortality rates

   **C** homelessness and inadequate housing

   **D** hunger and malnutrition

2 Which is a limitation of using real national income per capita as a measure of standards of living in a country?

   **A** It does not account for inflation over time.

   **B** It does not consider income earned in every industry.

   **C** It does not consider the size of the population.

   **D** It does not reflect the distribution of income and wealth.

3 Which is **not** part of the Human Development Index (HDI)?

   **A** education

   **B** environmental issues

   **C** healthcare

   **D** income levels

4 From the limited data below, which country is most likely to have the highest standard of living?

| Country | GDP ($ billion) | Population (million) |
|---------|-----------------|----------------------|
| A | 129.7 | 18.5 |
| B | 153.6 | 150.0 |
| C | 43.2 | 15.2 |
| D | 89.9 | 9.2 |

   **A** Country A

   **B** Country B

   **C** Country C

   **D** Country D

5 Which is **not** a direct criticism of using the Human Development Index (HDI) to classify countries?

   **A** Inequalities in income and wealth are ignored.

   **B** Longevity, education and income are not the only factors that affect human development.

   **C** The components of the HDI are indiscriminately weighted equally.

   **D** The definitions of economic development and standards of living are subjective.

 Cambridge IGCSE™ and O Level Economics 2nd edition Workbook

**6** Explain **two** reasons for differences in income distribution within countries. *[4 marks]*

..........................................................................................................................................

..........................................................................................................................................

..........................................................................................................................................

..........................................................................................................................................

..........................................................................................................................................

..........................................................................................................................................

**7** Dhaka in Bangladesh is rated by the Economics Intelligence Unit as one of the least liveable cities in the world. Explain **two** reasons why this might be the case. *[4 marks]*

..........................................................................................................................................

..........................................................................................................................................

..........................................................................................................................................

..........................................................................................................................................

..........................................................................................................................................

..........................................................................................................................................

**8** Explain **two** reasons why an increase in real GDP per capita may not result in a rise in living standards in a country. *[4 marks]*

..........................................................................................................................................

..........................................................................................................................................

..........................................................................................................................................

..........................................................................................................................................

..........................................................................................................................................

..........................................................................................................................................

**9** Economic growth is associated with an improvement in living standards.

**a** Define what is meant by *living standards*. *[2 marks]*

..........................................................................................................................

..........................................................................................................................

**b** Analyse **two** ways that a government can improve the living standards in its country. *[6 marks]*

..........................................................................................................................

..........................................................................................................................

..........................................................................................................................

..........................................................................................................................

..........................................................................................................................

..........................................................................................................................

..........................................................................................................................

**c** Discuss whether or not economic growth in a country always results in higher living standards for its people. *[8 marks]*

..........................................................................................................................

..........................................................................................................................

..........................................................................................................................

..........................................................................................................................

..........................................................................................................................

..........................................................................................................................

..........................................................................................................................

..........................................................................................................................

..........................................................................................................................

..........................................................................................................................

**10** Discuss which of the two countries below is most likely to have lower living standards based on the economic development indicators given in the table. *[8 marks]*

| Country | GDP per capita ($) | Life expectancy (years) | Expected years of schooling | Mean years of schooling |
|---|---|---|---|---|
| Guinea | 508 | 59 | 8.8 | 2.6 |
| Sierra Leone | 496 | 51 | 9.3 | 3.3 |

Source: World Bank (GDP per capita), UNDP (other data)

..........................................................................................................................

..........................................................................................................................

..........................................................................................................................

..........................................................................................................................

..........................................................................................................................

..........................................................................................................................

..........................................................................................................................

..........................................................................................................................

..........................................................................................................................

..........................................................................................................................

..........................................................................................................................

..........................................................................................................................

..........................................................................................................................

# 33 Poverty

**1** Which is least likely to be an indicator of poverty in an economy?

  **A** homelessness and inadequate housing     **C** inadequate income

  **B** hunger and malnutrition     **D** unemployment

**2** What exists when there is extreme outright poverty in an economy, i.e. average income is equal to or less than $1.25 per day?

  **A** absolute poverty     **C** poverty trap

  **B** poverty line     **D** relative poverty

**3** What is experienced by those who have a lower standard of living in comparison to the average member of society?

  **A** absolute poverty     **C** poverty trap

  **B** poverty line     **D** relative poverty

**4** Which is **not** a United Nations Sustainable Development Goal (SDG)?

  **A** clean water and sanitation     **C** reduced inequalities

  **B** reduce, reuse, recycle     **D** zero hunger

**5** Which is **least** likely to be a cause of poverty?

  **A** high public debt     **C** low GDP per capita

  **B** high rates of tax     **D** low literacy rates

**6** Use an example to explain the meaning of relative poverty.     *[2 marks]*

  ...................................................................................................................................................

  ...................................................................................................................................................

  ...................................................................................................................................................

**7** Study the data below and answer the questions that follow.

| Income ($ per year) | Tax paid per year ($) | | |
|---|---|---|---|
| | Tax A | Tax B | Tax C |
| 10 000 | 1000 | 650 | 500 |
| 15 000 | 1650 | 650 | 750 |
| 20 000 | 2400 | 650 | 1000 |
| 25 000 | 3250 | 650 | 1250 |

**a** Explain which tax (A, B or C) is progressive. *[2 marks]*

..................................................................................................................................

..................................................................................................................................

**b** Explain which tax (A, B or C) is proportional. *[2 marks]*

..................................................................................................................................

..................................................................................................................................

**c** Explain the difference between a regressive and a proportional tax. *[2 marks]*

..................................................................................................................................

..................................................................................................................................

**8** According to the World Bank, the GDP per capita in Mozambique was $392 in 2016 (just over $1 per day). Explain why poverty is a concern for the Mozambican government. *[4 marks]*

..................................................................................................................................

..................................................................................................................................

..................................................................................................................................

..................................................................................................................................

**9** Explain any **two** causes of poverty. *[4 marks]*

..................................................................................................................................

..................................................................................................................................

..................................................................................................................................

..................................................................................................................................

**10** Explain any **two** policies that can be used to alleviate poverty. *[4 marks]*

..................................................................................................................................

..................................................................................................................................

..................................................................................................................................

..................................................................................................................................

..................................................................................................................................

..................................................................................................................................

# 34 Population

1 Which factor is most likely to raise the average age of a population?

  **A**  a higher birth rate                **C**  improved health technologies

  **B**  a higher death rate               **D**  net migration

2 Which factor is likely to increase the population in a country?

  **A**  greater female participation in the workforce     **C**  higher fertility rates

  **B**  higher cost of living                   **D**  increased education expenditure

3 The net migration rate is calculated by the formula

  **A**  birth rate – death rate

  **B**  death rate – birth rate

  **C**  number of emigrants – number of immigrants

  **D**  number of immigrants – number of emigrants

4 Which statement about population distribution is correct?

  **A**  Low-income countries generally have a lower average age than high-income countries.

  **B**  Most countries are experiencing ageing populations.

  **C**  Poorer countries tend to have lower dependency ratios.

  **D**  The gender split is uneven in most countries with more females being born.

5 The median age of the UK population was 35.4 years in 1985 and is projected to be 42.2 by the year 2035. What does this suggest about the population in the UK?

  **A**  It has a declining birth rate.          **C**  It has a positive population growth rate.

  **B**  It has a declining death rate.         **D**  It has an ageing population.

6 Define the term *dependency ratio*.                          *[2 marks]*

......................................................................................................................

......................................................................................................................

......................................................................................................................

                                                                   *Cambridge IGCSE™ and O Level Economics 2nd edition Workbook*

**7** Explain **two** factors that affect the rate of population growth. *[4 marks]*

.......................................................................................................................................

.......................................................................................................................................

.......................................................................................................................................

.......................................................................................................................................

**8** Explain the difference between underpopulation and overpopulation. *[4 marks]*

.......................................................................................................................................

.......................................................................................................................................

.......................................................................................................................................

.......................................................................................................................................

**9** The chart below illustrates the growth in Mexico's population between 2006 and 2016.

**Mexico's population,** 2006–2016

Source: Trading Economics

**a** Explain what has happened to Mexico's population in the time period shown. *[2 marks]*

.......................................................................................................................................

.......................................................................................................................................

**b** Explain **two** economic problems which could be associated with the continual rise in the size of Mexico's population. *[4 marks]*

.......................................................................................................................................

.......................................................................................................................................

.......................................................................................................................................

.......................................................................................................................................

**c** Discuss whether or not the population growth will bring about negative consequences for the government and natural environment. *[8 marks]*

..........................................................................................

..........................................................................................

..........................................................................................

..........................................................................................

..........................................................................................

..........................................................................................

..........................................................................................

..........................................................................................

..........................................................................................

..........................................................................................

..........................................................................................

..........................................................................................

..........................................................................................

..........................................................................................

..........................................................................................

..........................................................................................

**10** Japan has an average age of 46.7 years whereas it is only 28.3 in Indonesia. The fertility rate is 1.42 in Japan and 2.42 in Indonesia. (Source: www.worldometers.info/world-population/)

**a** Define what is meant by an *ageing population*. *[2 marks]*

..........................................................................................

..........................................................................................

..........................................................................................

..........................................................................................

**b** Define what is meant by an *optimum population*. *[2 marks]*

...........................................................................................................................

...........................................................................................................................

...........................................................................................................................

...........................................................................................................................

**c** Analyse the impact of a high median age and low fertility rate on Japan's population structure. *[6 marks]*

...........................................................................................................................

...........................................................................................................................

...........................................................................................................................

...........................................................................................................................

...........................................................................................................................

...........................................................................................................................

...........................................................................................................................

...........................................................................................................................

**d** Analyse the impact of the low median age on Indonesia's dependency ratio. *[6 marks]*

...........................................................................................................................

...........................................................................................................................

...........................................................................................................................

...........................................................................................................................

...........................................................................................................................

...........................................................................................................................

...........................................................................................................................

# 35 Differences in economic development between countries

1 Which refers to an increase in the economic wellbeing and standard of living within a country?

   **A** economic development

   **B** economic growth

   **C** gross domestic product

   **D** production possibility frontier

2 Which factor does **not** account for differences in the economic development of countries?

   **A** exchange rate fluctuations

   **B** investment in education and healthcare

   **C** population growth

   **D** productivity levels

3 Which is least likely to be an indicator of economic development?

   **A** gender equality

   **B** greater self-esteem

   **C** higher interest rates

   **D** political freedom

4 Which sector of the economy do most people in less economically developed countries (LEDCs) tend to work in?

   **A** primary

   **B** public

   **C** secondary

   **D** tertiary

5 Attracting foreign direct investment (FDI) will enable a country to enjoy higher levels of what?

   **A** imports

   **B** productivity

   **C** savings

   **D** unemployment

6 Define the term *economic development*.                                            *[2 marks]*

   ........................................................................................................................................

   ........................................................................................................................................

7 With reference to investment in the economy, explain the importance of savings.        *[2 marks]*

   ........................................................................................................................................

   ........................................................................................................................................

   ........................................................................................................................................

*Cambridge IGCSE™ and O Level Economics 2nd edition Workbook*

**8** Explain how differences in population growth between countries have an impact on their level of economic development. *[4 marks]*

..............................................................................................................................

..............................................................................................................................

..............................................................................................................................

..............................................................................................................................

..............................................................................................................................

..............................................................................................................................

**9** As an economy develops, there tends to be a shift away from reliance on primary and secondary sector production. Explain why this is the case. *[4 marks]*

..............................................................................................................................

..............................................................................................................................

..............................................................................................................................

..............................................................................................................................

..............................................................................................................................

..............................................................................................................................

**10** Analyse how healthcare and education have a direct impact on a country's economic development. *[6 marks]*

..............................................................................................................................

..............................................................................................................................

..............................................................................................................................

..............................................................................................................................

..............................................................................................................................

..............................................................................................................................

..............................................................................................................................

..............................................................................................................................

# 36 International specialisation

1 Which is most likely to result from greater specialisation in manufacturing?

   **A** Consumers have more choice over individually made goods.

   **B** Employees benefit from greater job satisfaction.

   **C** Employees benefit from greater variety in the nature of their work.

   **D** Households benefit from lower prices.

2 Which is most likely to be a direct benefit of specialisation to workers in a specific industry?

   **A** employees becoming more skilled       **C** improved labour productivity

   **B** improved competitiveness       **D** reduced wastage

3 Which best explains why top Hollywood actors earn extremely high incomes?

   **A** It takes a relatively long time to train to become a top Hollywood actor.

   **B** There is a high supply of Hollywood actors.

   **C** There is low demand for Hollywood actors.

   **D** Top Hollywood actors work on one or two movies only each year.

4 Which is a disadvantage of international specialisation?

   **A** economies of scale       **C** improved international competitiveness

   **B** efficiency gains       **D** increased labour turnover

5 Which is an advantage of a high degree of international specialisation?

   **A** greater variety for consumers       **C** lower average costs

   **B** higher labour mobility       **D** lower labour mobility

6 With the use of relevant examples, explain what is meant by the term *specialisation*.    *[2 marks]*

........................................................................................................................................

........................................................................................................................................

........................................................................................................................................

........................................................................................................................................

**7** With the use of examples, explain how division of labour is a form of international specialisation. *[4 marks]*

..................................................................................................................

..................................................................................................................

..................................................................................................................

..................................................................................................................

**8** Explain **two** reasons why specialisation can lead to higher incomes for workers. *[4 marks]*

..................................................................................................................

..................................................................................................................

..................................................................................................................

..................................................................................................................

**9** Analyse why overspecialisation can be problematic for the economy. *[6 marks]*

..................................................................................................................

..................................................................................................................

..................................................................................................................

..................................................................................................................

..................................................................................................................

..................................................................................................................

**10** With the use of examples, discuss the advantages and disadvantages of international specialisation for firms. *[8 marks]*

..................................................................................................................

..................................................................................................................

..................................................................................................................

..................................................................................................................

..................................................................................................................

..................................................................................................................

..................................................................................................................

..................................................................................................................

# 37 Globalisation, free trade and protection

1 Which is an objective of trade protection?

   **A** to create domestic jobs

   **B** to improve the economic efficiency of domestic industries

   **C** to increase the demand for domestically produced goods and services

   **D** to reduce the costs of international trade

2 Which method of trade protection is used to directly reduce the price of exports?

   **A** embargoes       **B** quotas       **C** subsidies       **D** tariffs

3 What is the name given to the act of selling exports at artificially low prices, below those charged by domestic firms, and often less than the cost of production?

   **A** administrative barriers       **C** embargoes

   **B** dumping       **D** subsidies

4 International trade that takes place without any form of protection (barriers to international trade) is called

   **A** dumping.       **C** free trade.

   **B** exchange.       **D** international relations.

5 Which is **not** a benefit of free international trade and exchange?

   **A** choice       **C** efficiency gains

   **B** economies of scale       **D** transportation costs

6 Define the term *trade protection*.       *[2 marks]*

..............................................................................................................................................

..............................................................................................................................................

7 Explain **two** economic reasons why the USA might import fewer cars from the European Union.       *[4 marks]*

..............................................................................................................................................

..............................................................................................................................................

..............................................................................................................................................

..............................................................................................................................................

      *Cambridge IGCSE™ and O Level Economics 2nd edition Workbook*

**8** Explain **two** benefits to an economy that engages in free international trade.          *[4 marks]*

..............................................................................................................................

..............................................................................................................................

..............................................................................................................................

..............................................................................................................................

**9** Explain **two** methods that can be used to protect domestic industries from foreign competition.          *[4 marks]*

..............................................................................................................................

..............................................................................................................................

..............................................................................................................................

..............................................................................................................................

**10** Discuss whether the government should protect domestic industries from foreign competition.          *[8 marks]*

..............................................................................................................................

..............................................................................................................................

..............................................................................................................................

..............................................................................................................................

..............................................................................................................................

..............................................................................................................................

..............................................................................................................................

..............................................................................................................................

..............................................................................................................................

..............................................................................................................................

..............................................................................................................................

# 38 Foreign exchange rates

**1** Which is a drawback of using a fixed exchange rate system?

   **A** a fall in the demand for exports

   **B** a rise in the demand for imports

   **C** the large opportunity cost of using foreign exchange reserves to maintain the fixed rate

   **D** the uncertainty it creates for international trade and exchange

**2** In a floating exchange rate system, what is the name given to a rise in the value of an exchange rate?

   **A** appreciation                **C** devaluation

   **B** depreciation               **D** revaluation

**3** In which exchange rate system does the government intervene in the foreign exchange market to maintain its exchange rate at a predetermined level against other currencies?

   **A** devalued                   **C** floating

   **B** fixed                       **D** revalued

**4** In which exchange rate system is the exchange rate determined by the market forces of demand for and supply of the currency?

   **A** fixed                      **C** managed

   **B** floating                  **D** mixed

**5** With reference to the diagram below, identify the option that does **not** explain the change in the exchange rate of the New Zealand dollar.

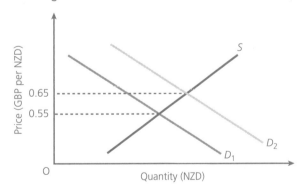

   **A** an increase in interest rates in New Zealand

   **B** greater demand from British households for New Zealand exports

   **C** more British tourists visiting New Zealand

   **D** more firms from New Zealand investing in Britain

**6** Define the term *exchange rate*. [2 marks]

..........................................................................................................................................

..........................................................................................................................................

**7** Suppose the exchange rate between the US dollar (USD) and the euro (EUR) is USD1 = EUR0.73.
Calculate the price for customers in Europe of buying textbooks priced at USD70 from the USA. [2 marks]

..........................................................................................................................................

..........................................................................................................................................

**8** Suppose the exchange rate between the British pound (GBP) and the Hong Kong dollar (HKD)
is GBP1 = HKD10.5. Calculate how much it costs a British tourist (in pounds) to buy an iPad
in Hong Kong that is priced at HKD6000. [2 marks]

..........................................................................................................................................

..........................................................................................................................................

**9** Suppose that the exchange rate between the Australian dollar (AUD) and the British pound
(GBP) is AUD1 = GBP0.57 while that between the Australian dollar and the Hong Kong dollar
(HKD) is AUD1 = HKD6. Calculate the exchange rate of the British pound against the
Hong Kong dollar. [2 marks]

..........................................................................................................................................

..........................................................................................................................................

**10** Although the Chinese government controls the value of its exchange rate, it has been known to allow
the yuan (the Chinese currency) to appreciate.

   **a** Explain what is meant by an appreciation in the value of a currency. [2 marks]

..........................................................................................................................................

..........................................................................................................................................

   **b** Analyse the likely effects of China's currency appreciation on its exports and imports. [6 marks]

..........................................................................................................................................

..........................................................................................................................................

..........................................................................................................................................

..........................................................................................................................................

..........................................................................................................................................

..........................................................................................................................................

..........................................................................................................................................

# 39 Current account of balance of payments

1 What is the name of the record of a country's exports and imports of physical goods?

    **A** the balance of payments     **C** the invisible trade balance

    **B** the current account     **D** the visible trade balance

2 What is **not** part of a country's net income flows and transfers?

    **A** bank deposits held in overseas banks     **C** money sent home from people working abroad

    **B** interest, profits and dividends     **D** money spent on intangible products

3 What is the correct formula for calculating a country's current account on the balance of payments?

    **A** trade balance + net exports

    **B** visible balance + invisible balance

    **C** visible trade balance + invisible trade balance + net income flows and transfers

    **D** visible trade balance + invisible trade balance – net income flows and transfers

4 What is a result of a sustained current account deficit for the domestic economy?

    **A** higher aggregate demand     **C** higher standards of living

    **B** higher exchange rate     **D** higher unemployment

5 Which policy is **least** likely to result in an improvement in the current account of the country?

    **A** lower exchange rate     **C** subsidies for export-driven firms

    **B** lower income taxes     **D** trade protection policies

6 Using the data below, describe what has happened to the country's balance of trade.   *[2 marks]*

| Year | Invisible balance ($bn) | Visible balance ($bn) |
|------|--------------------------|------------------------|
| 1 | 15.2 | 12.3 |
| 2 | 16.7 | 13.4 |

..................................................................................................................................................

..................................................................................................................................................

7 State any **two** components included in the current account of the balance of payments.   *[2 marks]*

..................................................................................................................................................

..................................................................................................................................................

**8** Explain how it is possible for a country to have a deficit on its visible trade balance
(trade in goods) but still have a current account surplus on its balance of payments. *[4 marks]*

.........................................................................................................................................

.........................................................................................................................................

.........................................................................................................................................

.........................................................................................................................................

**9** Study the data below and answer the questions that follow.

| Trade balance for Country D ($billion) | |
|---|---|
| **Exports** | 103 |
| Goods | 87 |
| Services | .......................................... |
| **Imports** | 113 |
| Goods | 87 |
| Services | .......................................... |
| Visible balance | .......................................... |
| Invisible balance | 10 |
| **Trade balance** | .......................................... |

**a** Define the term *visible balance*. *[2 marks]*

.........................................................................................................................................

.........................................................................................................................................

**b** Calculate the missing figures in the data above for Country D. *[2 marks]*

.........................................................................................................................................

.........................................................................................................................................

**10** Analyse how a fall in the exchange rate can reduce a country's current account deficit
on its balance of payments. *[6 marks]*

.........................................................................................................................................

.........................................................................................................................................

.........................................................................................................................................

.........................................................................................................................................

.........................................................................................................................................

.........................................................................................................................................

Reinforce learning and deepen understanding of the key concepts covered in the revised syllabus; an ideal course companion or homework book for use throughout the course.

» Develop and strengthen skills and knowledge with a wealth of additional exercises that perfectly supplement the Student's Book.

» Build confidence with extra practice for each lesson to ensure that a topic is thoroughly understood before moving on.

» Consolidate knowledge and skills with exercises based on authentic contexts and problems.

» Keep track of students' work with ready-to-go write-in exercises.

» Save time with all answers available online in the Online Teacher's Guide.

Use with *Cambridge IGCSE™ and O Level Economics 2nd edition*
9781510421271

**For over 30 years we have been trusted by Cambridge schools around the world to provide quality support for teaching and learning. For this reason we have been selected by Cambridge Assessment International Education as an official publisher of endorsed material for their syllabuses.**

Working for over
**30 YEARS**
WITH
Cambridge Assessment International Education

This resource is endorsed by Cambridge Assessment International Education

✓ Provides learner support for the Cambridge IGCSE™ and O Level Economics syllabuses (0455/2281) for examination from 2020

✓ Has passed Cambridge International's rigorous quality-assurance process

✓ Developed by subject experts

✓ For Cambridge schools worldwide

**HODDER** EDUCATION
e: education@hachette.co.uk
w: hoddereducation.com

ISBN 978-1-5104-2128-8

9 781510 421288

MIX
Paper | Supporting responsible forestry
FSC™ C104740